Sunshine

Mr Mole's Word Trainer 3

Erarbeitet von
Daniela Röbers und
Caroline Schröder

Unter Beratung von
Wolfgang Gehring und
Renate Hafner

Cornelsen

Contents

Symbols

read | write / draw / colour | extra

Du bist mit einem Kapitel fertig? Schneide das Bild dazu aus und klebe es hinten im Heft auf!

1 Read, number, draw and write.

☐ I'm fine, thanks!

1 Good morning! My name is Mr Mole. What's your name?

☐ How are you?

☐ My name is ______________.

This is me!

2 Read and draw lines. Find the extra speech bubble.

I'm fine, thanks.

I'm not very well.

I'm OK.

I'm cold.

How are you, Mr Mole?

zu 1: Nummeriere den Dialog in der richtigen Reihenfolge.
zu 2: Ordne die Sprechblasen den passenden Bildern zu und streiche die überflüssige Sprechblase durch. Wenn du möchtest, male Mr Mole an.

3 Find the words. Write the numbers.

T	W	O	Z	E	I	G	H	T	Q
W	B	T	D	G	O	S	K	H	L
E	S	E	V	E	N	I	O	R	P
L	A	N	G	T	A	X	I	E	U
V	U	R	O	N	E	Z	O	E	R
E	F	K	D	I	N	M	F	D	B
M	O	M	S	N	P	O	I	Y	T
X	U	A	T	E	L	E	V	E	N
P	R	W	J	C	F	S	E	V	G

	ten
	six
	eleven
	eight
	five
	two
	twelve
	four
	nine
1	one
	three
	seven

4 Write the words.

zu 3: Finde die Wörter im Suchworträtsel und schreibe die richtigen Zahlen dazu.
zu 4: Schreibe die Wörter passend zu den Zahlen im Bild auf.

1 Draw lines.

blue

orange

red

green

black

grey

pink

white

yellow

brown

2 Write.

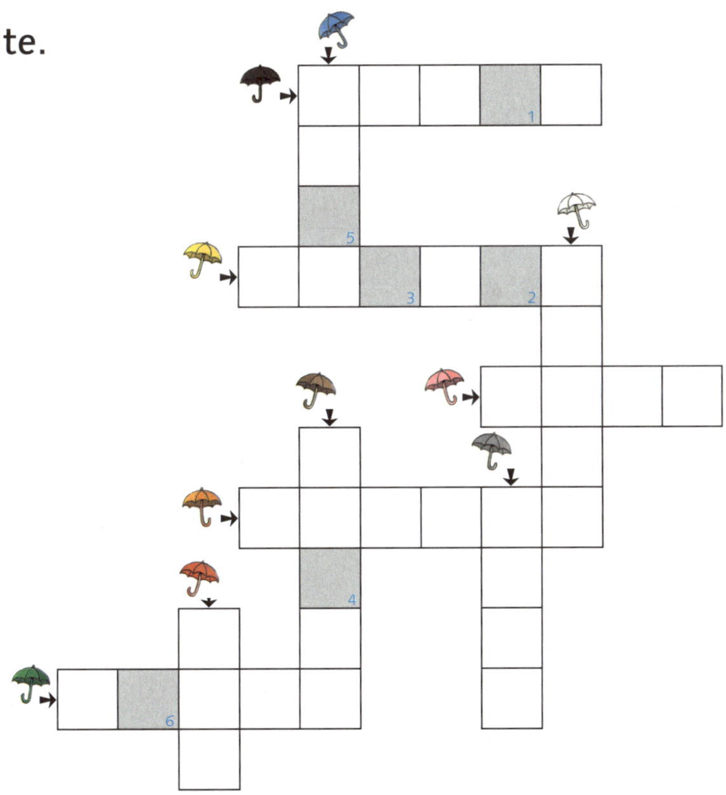

Solution:

I like all _ _ _ _ _ _ S !

1 2 3 4 5 6

zu 1: Verbinde die Wörter mit den passenden Bildern.
zu 2: Schreibe die (Farb-)Wörter auf und finde das Lösungswort.

3 Find the words.

→ ↓

R	E	D	G	B	L	U	E	N	G
Z	L	D	T	L	N	M	Y	X	R
O	R	W	E	A	W	B	E	D	E
R	Q	H	B	C	F	R	L	X	Y
A	P	I	N	K	T	R	L	P	W
N	A	T	W	A	B	R	O	W	N
G	R	E	E	N	V	S	W	F	U
E	H	K	D	U	T	I	P	Z	E

black · blue · brown · green · grey · orange · pink · red · white · yellow

4 Count, write and draw.

five blue umbrellas

six ______ lollipops

______ ______ T-shirts

______ ______ skateboards

______ ______ toasts

______ ______ ______

______ ______ ______

zu 3: Finde die Wörter im Suchworträtsel.
zu 4: Schreibe die Wörter, die zu den Bildern passen, auf. Male eigene Bilder zu Wörtern, die du kennst und schreibe diese auf.

5 Read and tick (✓). Write.

The mountain bike is
- ☐ green.
- ☐ white.
- ☐ brown.

The in-line skates are
- ☐ grey and orange.
- ☐ black and white.
- ☐ blue and black.

The scooter is
- ☐ green and blue.
- ☐ yellow and white.
- ☐ green and yellow.

The ____________ is
- ☐ grey, blue and yellow.
- ☐ red, blue and orange.
- ☐ black, green and orange.

6 Read and colour.

red	blue	white	yellow
pink	grey	yellow	green
black	brown	blue	red
green	orange	black	brown

zu 5: Finde heraus, wie die Sätze richtig heißen und hake ab.
Schreibe das fehlende Wort auf.
zu 6: Male die Farbklekse passend zu den (Farb-)Wörtern an.

7 Number.

5 sister	☐ brother	☐ grandfather
☐ father	☐ grandmother	☐ mother

8 Write.

h r d g f r a t n a e	grandfather
o r t e m h	
d n r o h m r g t e a	
e r t b h o r	
t s r s e i	
e f h t r a	

zu 7: Nummeriere die Wörter passend zum Bild.
zu 8: Ordne die Buchstaben und schreibe die (Familien-)Wörter richtig auf.

9 Find the family words.

10 Write.

brother · brothers · father · grandfather · grandmother · mother · sister

I've got
a ______________________,
a ______________________ and
a ____________________.

I've got
a ______________________,
a ______________________ and
two ____________________.

I've got
a ______________________,
a ______________________,
a ______________________ and
a ____________________.

zu 9: Finde die (Familien-)Wörter in der Wortschlange und umkreise sie.
zu 10: Ergänze die Sprechblasen mit den zu den Bildern passenden (Familien-)Wörtern.

11 Read and write.

name: Mr Mole

family: mother, father,
2 grandmothers, 2 grandfathers,
1 brother, 1 sister

♥ **colour:** red

best friend: Mr Digger

Linda: Hi, I'm Linda. What's your name?

Mr Mole: Hi, my name is ________.

Linda: Have you got a brother or a sister?

Mr Mole: I've got ________ and ________.

Linda: What's your favourite colour?

Mr Mole: My favourite colour is ________.

Linda: Who is your best friend?

Mr Mole: My best friend is ________.

Read and tick (✓).

It's ☐ Ben's ☐ Paul's family.

zu 11: Lies Mr Moles Steckbrief und ergänze die Sätze.
zu Extra: Finde den zum Bild passenden Text und hake den richtigen Namen ab.

Pets in the garden

1 Draw lines.

dog

guinea pig

fish

rat

rabbit

hamster

frog

cat

mouse

2 Find the words. Circle and write.

sunshine
sunshinesunshine
sunshinesunshinesunshine
sunshineguinea pigsunshine
sunshinemousesunshinesunshine
sunshinefrogsunshinecatsunshine
sunshinesunshinesunshinesunshine
sunshinesunshineratsunshinesunshine
sunshinehamstersunshinesunshine
sunshinefishsunshinedogsunshine
sunshinerabbitsunshine
sunshinesunshine
sunshine

fish

3 Write.

g d o		a r t e h s m	
a t r		b a r b t i	
s i f h		s o e m u	
t c a		u i g n a e g p i	

4 Find the pets. Write.

Sally has got a ______________.

______________.

______________.

______________.

zu 3: Ordne die Buchstaben und schreibe die (Tier-)Wörter richtig auf.
zu 4: Fahre die Linien nach und schreibe auf, welche Haustiere zu den Kindern gehören.

Pets in the garden

5 Read and tick (✓).

Kate has got a
- ☐ red hamster.
- ☐ brown cat.
- ☐ brown hamster.

Emily has got a
- ☐ grey and brown dog.
- ☐ black and white cat.
- ☐ black and white mouse.

Samir has got a
- ☐ white and yellow guinea pig.
- ☐ brown and white guinea pig.
- ☐ brown and white rabbit.

Harry has got a
- ☐ blue rat and a black dog
- ☐ white mouse and a brown cat.
- ☐ white rabbit and a grey and white rat.

6 Read, colour and write.

There are three red rabbits.
There is one green mouse.
There are seven grey fish.

There are four blue hamsters.
There are five orange dogs.
There are six brown cats.

How many white pets are there? There are ______ white pets.

zu 5: Finde heraus, wie die Sätze richtig heißen und hake ab.
zu 6: Lies die Sätze und male die Tiere passend zu den Aussagen an. Schreibe auf, wie viele Tiere weiß bleiben.

7 Number.

☐	☐	1
		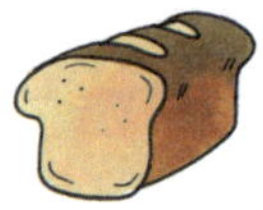
☐	☐	☐

1 carrot
2 apple
3 peanuts
4 lettuce
5 tomato
6 bread

8 Read, colour and write.

There are nine green carrots.

There are six orange peanuts.

There are five brown tomatoes.

There are ________ blue ____________.

________ is ____________ yellow lettuce.

zu 7: Nummeriere die Bilder passend zu den Wörtern.
zu 8: Lies die Sätze und ergänze sie passend zum Bild. Male die Bilder passend zu den Aussagen an.

9 Write. Find the extra words.

hamster · carrot · dog · peanut · mouse · ~~fish~~ · red · cat · rabbit · rat · water · lettuce · bread · guinea pig · tomato · (jeans) · apple

pets

fish, ____
____
____
____

food

____
____
____
____

Jeans, ____ and ____ are extra.

10 Write and draw.

There are five carrots. 

____ ____ three tomatoes. 

____ ____ six ____. 

____ ____ ____ apples. 

There is ____ ____. 

____ ____ ____ ____. 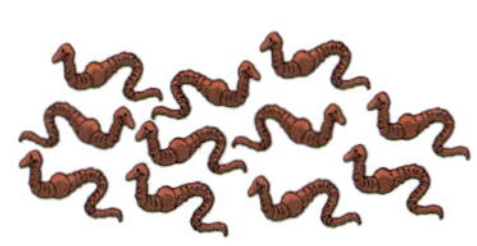

zu 9: Ordne die Wörter den richtigen Wortfeldern zu und schreibe sie auf. Umkreise die überflüssigen Wörter und schreibe sie auf.
zu 10: Ergänze die Sätze und male das fehlende Bild.

11 Write.

My favourite pet
is a ______________.
Its name is ______________.
It likes ______________.
It is brown.

My favourite pet
is ______________.
Its ______________.
It ______________.
______________.

Right or wrong? Tick (✓). Write.

	right	wrong
Rabbits like popcorn.		✓
Hamsters like peanuts.		
Fish like bread.		
Dogs like tomatoes.		
Cats like carrots.		
Rats like apples.		

Right answer:

Rabbits like ______________.

zu 11: Ergänze die Sprechblasen.
zu Extra: Entscheide, ob eine Aussage richtig oder falsch ist und hake an der richtigen Stelle ab. Finde heraus, was Kaninchen fressen und ergänze den Satz mit dem richtigen Wort.

1 Draw lines.

pencil
felt tip
pencil case
glue stick
pencil sharpener
ruler

lunch box
rubber
school bag
pen
scissors
book

2 Write.

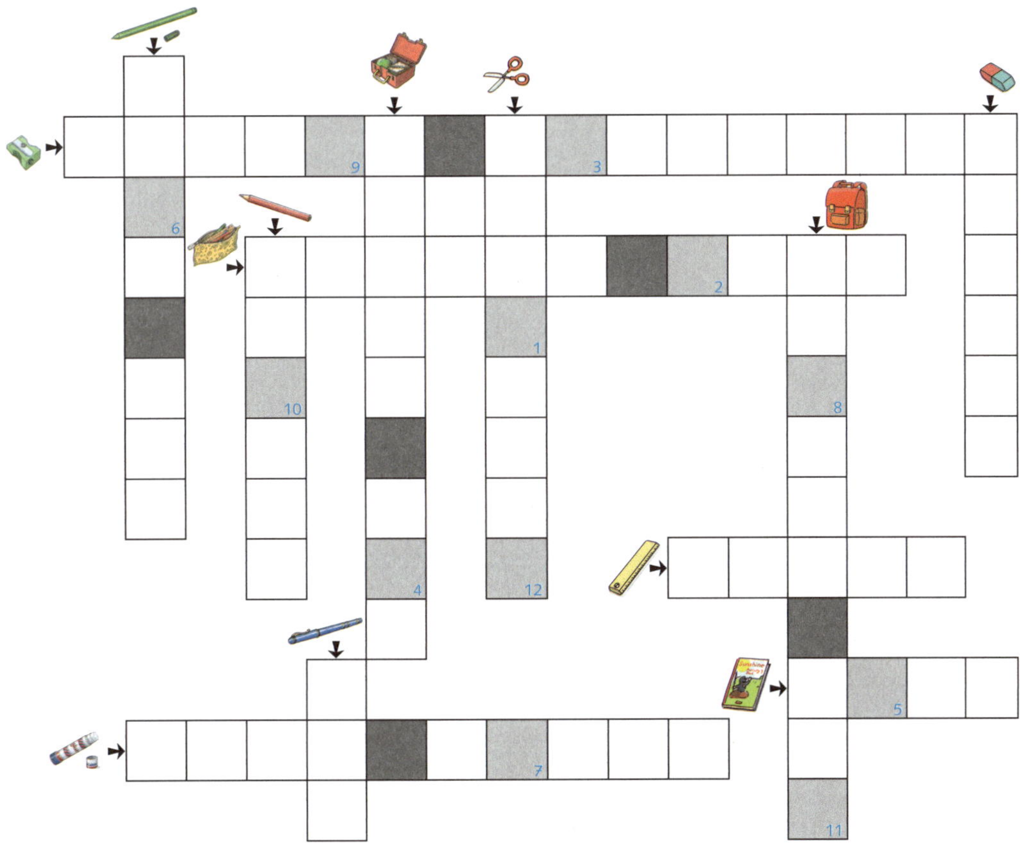

Solution:

1	2	3	4	5	6		7	8	9	10	11	12

zu 1: Verbinde die Wörter mit den passenden Bildern.
zu 2: Schreibe die (Schulsachen-)Wörter auf. Finde das Lösungswort.

3 Find the school things. Tick (✓). What's missing?

- [x] felt tip
- [ ] book
- [ ] glue stick
- [ ] lunch box
- [ ] pencil case
- [ ] pencil sharpener
- [ ] rubber
- [ ] ruler
- [ ] school bag
- [ ] scissors

The ________________ is missing.

4 Find the words. Write.

→ ↓

R	S	C	H	O	O	L		B	A	G	Y	Q	F	K	G
O	L	P	T	P	E	N	C	I	L		C	A	S	E	N
N	F	E	L	T		T	I	P	M	R	U	B	B	E	R
P	E	N	C	I	L		S	H	A	R	P	E	N	E	R
E	Y	C	G	P	I	P	K	T	B	C	P	Y	Y	Y	U
N	Y	I	E	S	C	I	S	S	O	R	S	D	Y	W	L
U	E	L	U	N	C	H		B	O	X	F	M	P	R	E
G	L	U	E		S	T	I	C	K	T	L	U	O	Z	R

 ________________  ________________  ________________

 ________________  ________________  ________________

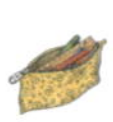 ________________  ________________  ________________

 ________________  ________________  ________________

zu 3: Lies die Wörter und finde die Gegenstände dazu im Bild. Hake ab. Schreibe auf, welcher Gegenstand im Bild fehlt.
zu 4: Finde die Wörter im Suchworträtsel und schreibe sie auf.

5 Write.

nclipe	left itp
kobo	plncei scea
urerl	cilpen harsnrepe
ebrrbu	elgu itskc
nep	hclnu oxb
ocsissrs	osolhc gba

6 Find the school words. Write the missing word.

The word ____________ is missing.

zu 5: Ordne die Buchstaben und schreibe die (Schulsachen-)Wörter richtig auf.
zu 6: Finde die Wörter und umkreise sie. Schreibe den fehlenden Schulgegenstand auf.

7 Count and write.

books · glue sticks · lunch boxes · pens · pencils · ~~pencil cases~~ · rubbers · rulers · scissors · school bag

There are 4 pencil cases. ______.

There are ______. ______.

There ______. ______.

______. There is ______.

______. There are no ______.

8 Write.

Can I have ..., please? · Yes, you can. Here you are. · Sorry, I haven't got a ...

zu 7: Zähle die Gegenstände und schreibe Sätze dazu.
zu 8: Ergänze die Sprechblasen.

9 Draw lines. Find the extra word.

draw

circle

write

colour

listen

read

talk

The word ______________ is extra.

10 Read and do.

1. Circle Mr Mole.
2. Colour Mr Mole yellow and his T-shirt green.
3. Draw a school bag.
4. Colour the school bag red.
5. Write Mr Mole's name.
6. Write your name.

name: ______________

My name is ______________.

zu 9: Verbinde die Wörter mit den richtigen Bildern. Umkreise das überflüssige Wort und schreibe es auf.
zu 10: Lies die Sätze und setze die Aktivitäten um.

11 Number.

1. behind
2. next to
3. on
4. under
5. in front of
6. in

Write and tick (✓).

Mr Mole is ______ the ☐ pencil case. ☐ rubber. ☐ ruler.

Mr Mole is ______ the ☐ school bag. ☐ ruler. ☐ pencil sharpener.

Mr Mole is ______ the ☐ school bag. ☐ book. ☐ pencil sharpener.

Mr Mole is ______ the ______.

Mr Mole is ______ the ______.

Mr Mole is ______ the ______.

zu 11: Nummeriere die Bilder passend zu den Wörtern.
zu Extra: Finde heraus, wie die Sätze richtig heißen und hake ab. Schreibe die fehlenden Wörter auf. Schreibe die letzten drei Sätze vollständig auf.

1 Draw lines. Find the extra word.

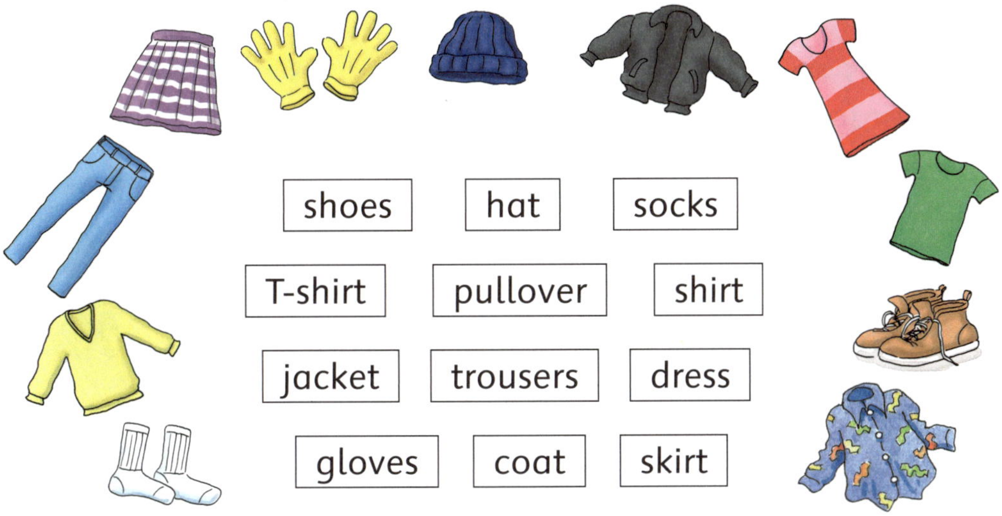

shoes	hat	socks
T-shirt	pullover	shirt
jacket	trousers	dress
gloves	coat	skirt

The word ______________ is extra.

2 Find the words. Write.

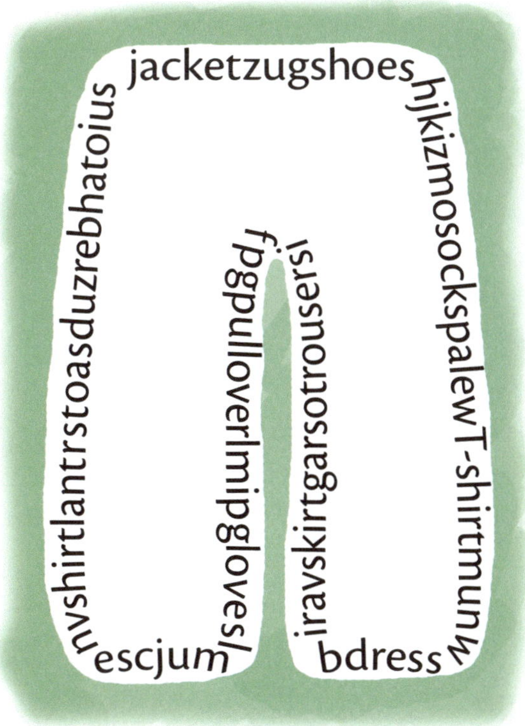

trousers
gloves
skirt
pullover
dress
shirt
socks
T-shirt
shoes
jacket
hat

zu 1: Verbinde die Wörter mit den passenden Bildern. Umkreise das überflüssige Wort und schreibe es auf.
zu 2: Finde die Wörter zu den Abbildungen, umkreise und schreibe sie auf.

3 Read and colour.

Kate is wearing an orange jacket, blue trousers and green gloves.

Samir is wearing a yellow jacket, green shoes and a grey hat.

Harry is wearing a black hat, yellow gloves, and red trousers.

Emily is wearing a green jacket, brown shoes and a pink pullover.

4 One word is wrong. Circle and write.

socks	blue	shirt	hat	blue
yellow	pink	skirt	green	
hat	grey	shirt	shoes	
shirt	green	yellow	white	
trousers	jacket	pullover	brown	
jeans	black	T-shirt	cap	

zu 3: Lies die Texte und male die Kleidungsstücke der Kinder dazu passend an.
zu 4: Umkreise in jeder Zeile das nicht passende Wort und schreibe es auf.

Liebe Schülerin, lieber Schüler,

auf den folgenden Seiten findest du die Lösungen zu deinen Aufgaben.

- Wenn du mit einer Seite oder einem Kapitel fertig bist, kannst du deine Ergebnisse selbstständig kontrollieren und, wenn nötig, verbessern.
- Damit du dir deine Wörter noch besser merken kannst, findest du weiter hinten hilfreiche Tipps, mit denen das Lernen Spaß macht. Dort hast du auch Platz für deine eigenen Notizen und zum weiteren Üben.
- Du kannst den Lösungsteil auch herausnehmen und zu Hause oder in der Schule aufbewahren.

Lösungen:

Getting started
saying hello

1 Read, number, draw and write.

4 I'm fine, thanks!

1 Good morning! My name is Mr Mole. What's your name?

3 How are you?

2 My name is ________.

This is me!

2 Read and draw lines. Find the extra speech bubble.

I'm fine, thanks.

I'm not very well.

I'm OK.

I'm cold.

How are you, Mr Mole?

zu 1: Nummeriere den Dialog in der richtigen Reihenfolge.
zu 2: Ordne die Sprechblasen den passenden Bildern zu und streiche die überflüssige Sprechblase durch. Wenn du möchtest, male Mr Mole an.

three 3

3 Find the words. Write the numbers.

T	W	O	Z	E	I	G	H	T	Q
W	B	T	D	G	O	S	K	H	L
E	S	E	V	E	N	I	O	R	P
L	A	N	G	T	A	X	I	E	U
V	U	R	O	N	E	Z	O	E	R
E	F	K	D	I	N	M	F	D	B
M	O	M	S	N	P	O	I	Y	T
X	U	A	T	E	L	E	V	E	N
P	R	W	J	C	F	S	E	V	G

- 10 ten
- 6 six
- 11 eleven
- 8 eight
- 5 five
- 2 two
- 12 twelve
- 4 four
- 9 nine
- 1 one
- 3 three
- 7 seven

4 Write the words.

three two seven nine

five six four one eight ten

11 eleven 12 twelve

zu 3: Finde die Wörter im Suchworträtsel und schreibe die richtigen Zahlen dazu.
zu 4: Schreibe die Wörter passend zu den Zahlen im Bild auf.

1 Draw lines.

blue · orange · red · green · black

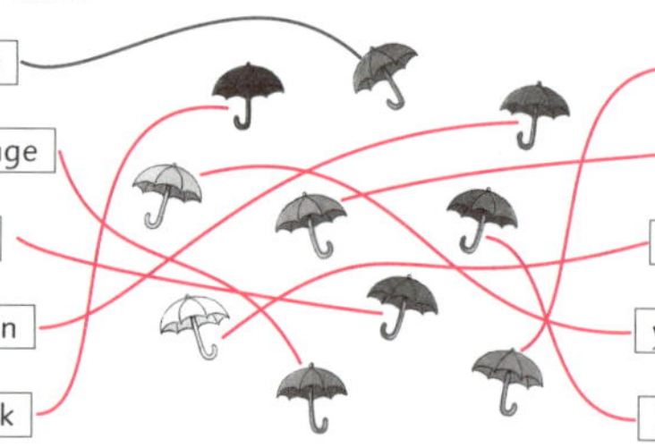

grey · pink · white · yellow · brown

2 Write.

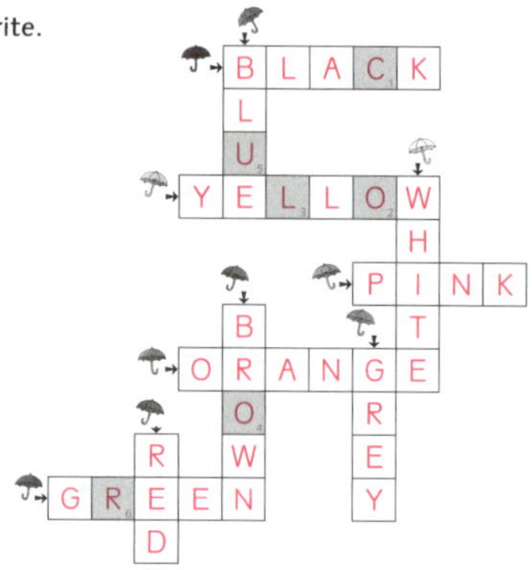

Solution:

I like all COLOURS !

zu 1: Verbinde die Wörter mit den passenden Bildern.
zu 2: Schreibe die (Farb-)Wörter auf und finde das Lösungswort.

3 Find the words.

R	E	D	G	B	L	U	E	N	G
Z	L	D	T	L	N	M	Y	X	R
O	R	W	E	A	W	B	E	D	E
R	Q	H	B	C	F	R	L	X	Y
A	P	I	N	K	T	R	L	P	W
N	A	T	W	A	B	R	O	W	N
G	R	E	E	N	V	S	W	F	U
E	H	K	D	U	T	I	P	Z	E

black · blue · brown · green · grey · orange · pink · red · white · yellow

4 Count, write and draw.

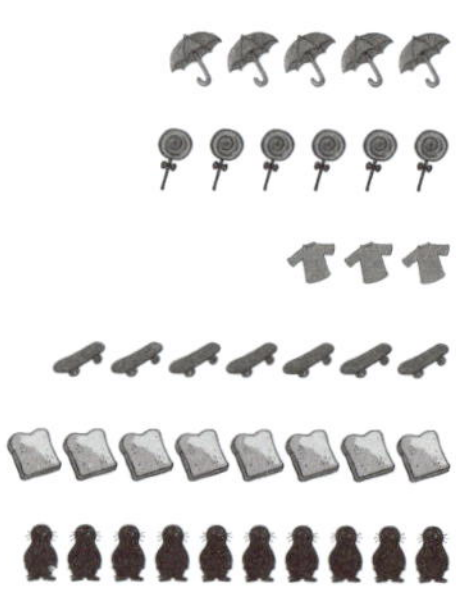

five blue umbrellas

six green lollipops

three orange T-shirts

seven red skateboards

eight brown toasts

ten black moles

zu 3: Finde die Wörter im Suchworträtsel.
zu 4: Schreibe die Wörter, die zu den Bildern passen, auf. Male eigene Bilder zu Wörtern, die du kennst und schreibe diese auf.

5 Read and tick (✓). Write.

The mountain bike is
- [x] green.
- [ ] white.
- [ ] brown.

The in-line skates are
- [ ] grey and orange.
- [ ] black and white.
- [x] blue and black.

The scooter is
- [ ] green and blue.
- [ ] yellow and white.
- [x] green and yellow.

The skateboard is
- [ ] grey, blue and yellow.
- [x] red, blue and orange.
- [ ] black, green and orange.

6 Read and colour.

red	blue	white	yellow
pink	grey	yellow	green
black	brown	blue	red
green	orange	black	brown

zu 5: Finde heraus, wie die Sätze richtig heißen und hake ab. Schreibe das fehlende Wort auf.
zu 6: Male die Farbkleckse passend zu den (Farb-)Wörtern an.

7 Number.

5 sister	6 brother	1 grandfather
4 father	2 grandmother	3 mother

8 Write.

h r d g f r a t n a e	grandfather
o r t e m h	mother
d n r o h m r g t e a	grandmother
e r t b h o r	brother
t s r s e i	sister
e f h t r a	father

zu 7: Nummeriere die Wörter passend zum Bild.
zu 8: Ordne die Buchstaben und schreibe die (Familien-)Wörter richtig auf.

9 Find the family words.

10 Write.

brother · brothers · father · grandfather · grandmother · mother · sister

I've got a father, a mother and a sister.

I've got a mother, a grandmother and two brothers.

I've got a brother, a sister, a mother and a father.

zu 9: Finde die (Familien-)Wörter in der Wortschlange und umkreise sie.
zu 10: Ergänze die Sprechblasen mit den zu den Bildern passenden (Familien-)Wörtern.

11 Read and write.

name: Mr Mole

family: mother, father, 2 grandmothers, 2 grandfathers, 1 brother, 1 sister

♥ **colour:** red

best friend: Mr Digger

Linda: Hi, I'm Linda. What's your name?
Mr Mole: Hi, my name is Mr Mole.
Linda: Have you got a brother or a sister?
Mr Mole: I've got 1 brother and 1 sister.
Linda: What's your favourite colour?
Mr Mole: My favourite colour is red.
Linda: Who is your best friend?
Mr Mole: My best friend is Mr Digger.

☆ Read and tick (✓).

Hello, my name is Ben. In the picture you can see me with my father, my mother and my grandmother.

My name is Paul. This is me with my mother, my father, my grandmother, my grandfather and my sister, Jenny.

It's ☑ Ben's ☐ Paul's family.

zu 11: Lies Mr Moles Steckbrief und ergänze die Sätze.
zu Extra: Finde den zum Bild passenden Text und hake den richtigen Namen ab.

1 Draw lines.

dog
guinea pig
fish
rat

rabbit
hamster
frog
cat
mouse

2 Find the words. Circle and write.

sunshine
sunshinesunshine
sunshinesunshinesunshine
sunshineguinea pigsunshine
sunshinemousesunshinesunshine
sunshinefrogsunshinecatsunshine
sunshinesunshinesunshinesunshine
sunshinesunshineratsunshinesunshine
sunshinehamstersunshinesunshine
sunshinefishsunshinedogsunshine
sunshinerabbitsunshine
sunshinesunshine
sunshine

cat
rabbit
mouse
hamster
fish
dog
frog
guinea pig
rat

zu 1: Verbinde die Wörter mit den passenden Bildern.
zu 2: Finde die (Tier-)Wörter, umkreise und schreibe sie auf.

3 Write.

g d o	dog	a r t e h s m	hamster
a t r	rat	b a r b t i	rabbit
s i f h	fish	s o e m u	mouse
t c a	cat	u i g n a e g p i	guinea pig

4 Find the pets. Write.

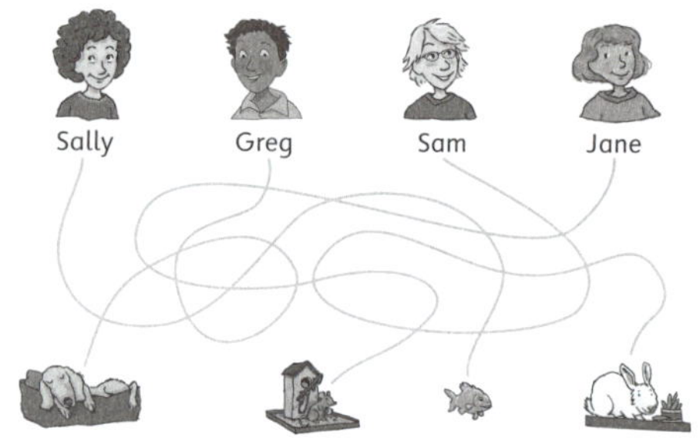

Sally has got a fish.
Greg has got a dog.
Sam has got a rabbit.
Jane has got a mouse.

zu 3: Ordne die Buchstaben und schreibe die (Tier-)Wörter richtig auf.
zu 4: Fahre die Linien nach und schreibe auf, welche Haustiere zu den Kindern gehören.

5 Read and tick (✓).

Kate has got a
- [ ] red hamster.
- [ ] brown cat.
- [x] brown hamster.

Emily has got a
- [ ] grey and brown dog.
- [x] black and white cat.
- [ ] black and white mouse.

Samir has got a
- [ ] white and yellow guinea pig.
- [x] brown and white guinea pig.
- [ ] brown and white rabbit.

Harry has got a
- [ ] blue rat and a black dog
- [ ] white mouse and a brown cat.
- [x] white rabbit and a grey and white rat.

6 Read, colour and write.

There are three red rabbits.
There is one green mouse.
There are seven grey fish.
There are four blue hamsters.
There are five orange dogs.
There are six brown cats.

How many white pets are there? There are seven white pets.

zu 5: Finde heraus, wie die Sätze richtig heißen und hake ab.
zu 6: Lies die Sätze und male die Tiere passend zu den Aussagen an. Schreibe auf, wie viele Tiere weiß bleiben.

7 Number.

 4
 5
 1
 2
 3
 6

1. carrot
2. apple
3. peanuts
4. lettuce
5. tomato
6. bread

8 Read, colour and write.

There are nine green carrots.
There are six orange peanuts.
There are five brown tomatoes.
There are three blue apples.
There is one yellow lettuce.

zu 7: Nummeriere die Bilder passend zu den Wörtern.
zu 8: Lies die Sätze und ergänze sie passend zum Bild. Male die Bilder passend zu den Aussagen an.

9 Write. Find the extra words.

hamster · carrot · dog · peanut · mouse · ~~fish~~ · (red) · cat · rabbit · rat · (water) · lettuce · bread · guinea pig · tomato · (jeans) · apple

pets
fish, hamster, dog, mouse, cat, rabbit, rat, guinea pig

food
carrot, peanut, lettuce, bread, tomato, apple

Jeans, red and water are extra.

10 Write and draw.

There are five carrots. 
There are three tomatoes. 
There are six peanuts. 
There are four apples. 
There is one lettuce. 
There are eleven worms. 

zu 9: Ordne die Wörter den richtigen Wortfeldern zu und schreibe sie auf. Umkreise die überflüssigen Wörter und schreibe sie auf.
zu 10: Ergänze die Sätze und male das fehlende Bild.

11 Write.

My favourite pet is a hamster.
Its name is Billy.
It likes peanuts.
It is brown.

My favourite pet is a rabbit.
Its name is Molly.
It likes carrots.
It is white.

Right or wrong? Tick (✓). Write.

	right	wrong
Rabbits like popcorn.		✓
Hamsters like peanuts.	✓	
Fish like bread.	✓	
Dogs like tomatoes.		✓
Cats like carrots.		✓
Rats like apples.	✓	

Right answer:

Rabbits like carrots.

zu 11: Ergânze die Sprechblasen.
zu Extra: Entscheide, ob eine Aussage richtig oder falsch ist und hake an der richtigen Stelle ab. Finde heraus, was Kaninchen fressen und ergänze den Satz mit dem richtigen Wort.

1 Draw lines.

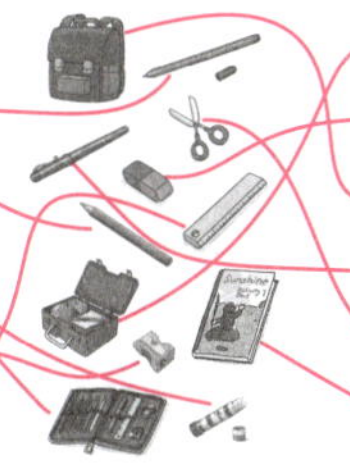

2 Write.

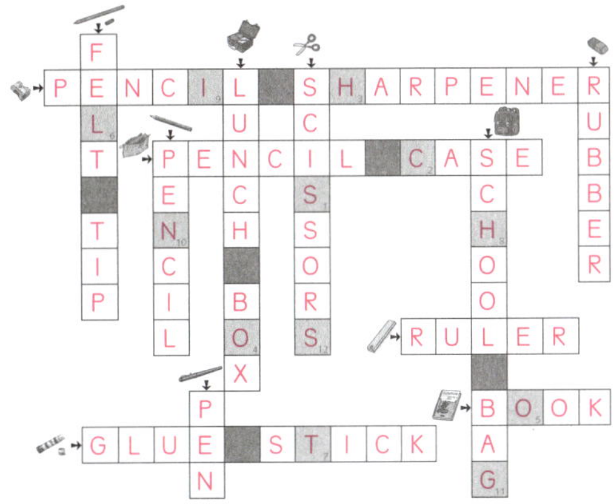

Solution:

1	2	3	4	5	6		7	8	9	10	11	12
S	C	H	O	O	L		T	H	I	N	G	S

zu 1: Verbinde die Wörter mit den passenden Bildern.
zu 2: Schreibe die (Schulsachen-)Wörter auf. Finde das Lösungswort.

3 Find the school things. Tick (✓).
What's missing?

- ☑ felt tip
- ☑ book
- ☑ glue stick
- ☐ lunch box
- ☑ pencil case
- ☑ pencil sharpener
- ☑ rubber
- ☑ ruler
- ☑ school bag
- ☑ scissors

The lunch box is missing.

4 Find the words. Write.

R	S	C	H	O	O	L		B	A	G	Y	Q	F	K	G
O	L	P	T	P	E	N	C	I	L		C	A	S	E	N
N	F	E	L	T		T	I	P	M	R	U	B	B	E	R
P	E	N	C	I	L		S	H	A	R	P	E	N	E	R
E	Y	C	G	P	I	P	K	T	B	C	P	Y	Y	Y	U
N	Y	I	E	S	C	I	S	S	O	R	S	D	Y	W	L
U	E	L	U	N	C	H		B	O	X	F	M	P	R	E
G	L	U	E		S	T	I	C	K	T	L	U	O	Z	R

- lunch box
- pencil sharpener
- pencil case
- school bag
- book
- rubber
- ruler
- pen
- scissors
- pencil
- felt tip
- glue stick

zu 3: Lies die Wörter und finde die Gegenstände dazu im Bild. Hake ab. Schreibe auf, welcher Gegenstand im Bild fehlt.
zu 4: Finde die Wörter im Suchworträtsel und schreibe sie auf.

5 Write.

nclipe	pencil	lefttip	felt tip
kobo	book	plncei scea	pencil case
urerl	ruler	cilpen harsnrepe	pencil sharpener
ebrrbu	rubber	elgu itskc	glue stick
nep	pen	hclnu oxb	lunch box
ocsisssrs	scissors	osolhc gba	school bag

6 Find the school words. Write the missing word.

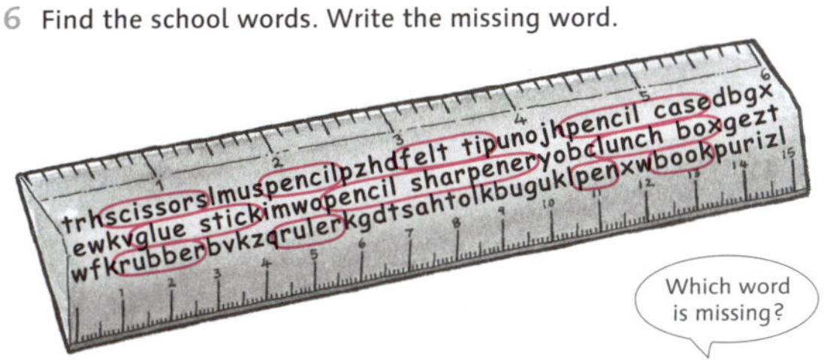

The word school bag is missing.

zu 5: Ordne die Buchstaben und schreibe die (Schulsachen)Wörter richtig auf.
zu 6: Finde die Wörter und umkreise sie. Schreibe den fehlenden Schulgegenstand auf.

7 Count and write.

books · glue sticks · lunch boxes · pens · pencils · ~~pencil cases~~ · rubbers · rulers · scissors · school bag

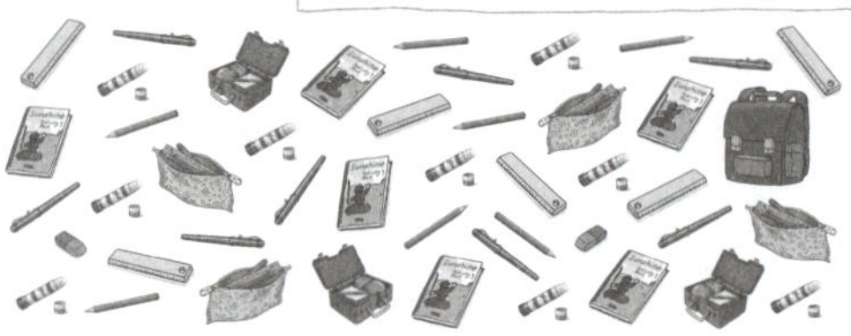

There are 4 pencil cases. There are 7 pencils.
There are 6 books. There are 2 rubbers.
There are 3 lunch boxes. There are 6 rulers.
There are 9 glue sticks. There is 1 school bag.
There are 8 pens. There are no scissors.

8 Write.

Can I have …, please? · Yes, you can. Here you are. · Sorry, I haven't got a …

zu 7: Zähle die Gegenstände und schreibe Sätze dazu.
zu 8: Ergänze die Sprechblasen.

9 Draw lines. Find the extra word.

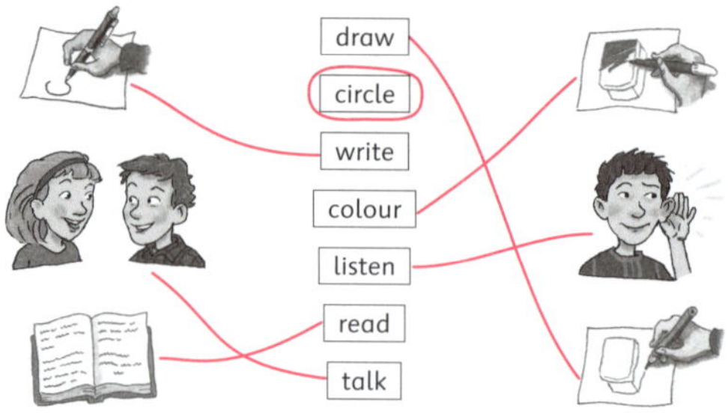

The word circle is extra.

10 Read and do.

1. Circle Mr Mole.
2. Colour Mr Mole yellow and his T-shirt green.
3. Draw a school bag.
4. Colour the school bag red.
5. Write Mr Mole's name.
6. Write your name.

name: Mr Mole

My name is ______.

zu 9: Verbinde die Wörter mit den richtigen Bildern. Umkreise das überflüssige Wort und schreibe es auf.
zu 10: Lies die Sätze und setze die Aktivitäten um.

11 Number.

1. behind
2. next to
3. on
4. under
5. in front of
6. in

Write and tick (✓).

Mr Mole is on the ☐ pencil case. ☑ rubber. ☐ ruler.

Mr Mole is in the ☑ school bag. ☐ ruler. ☐ pencil sharpener.

Mr Mole is under the ☐ school bag. ☑ book. ☐ pencil sharpener.

Mr Mole is next to the ruler.

Mr Mole is in front of the pencil case.

Mr Mole is behind the pencil sharpener.

zu 11: Nummeriere die Bilder passend zu den Wörtern.
zu Extra: Finde heraus, wie die Sätze richtig heißen und hake ab. Schreibe die fehlenden Wörter auf. Schreibe die letzten drei Sätze vollständig auf.

1 Draw lines. Find the extra word.

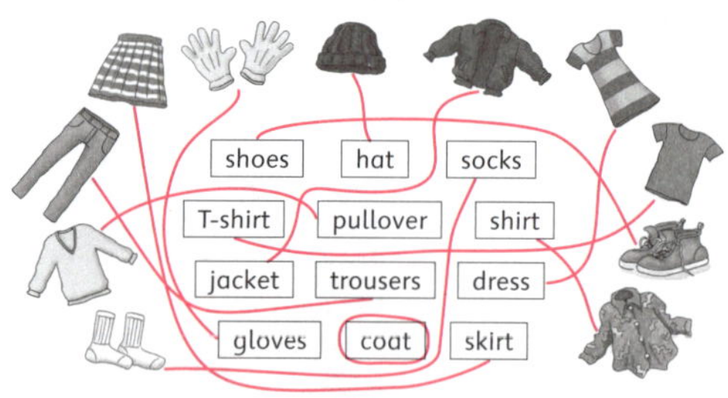

The word coat is extra.

2 Find the words. Write.

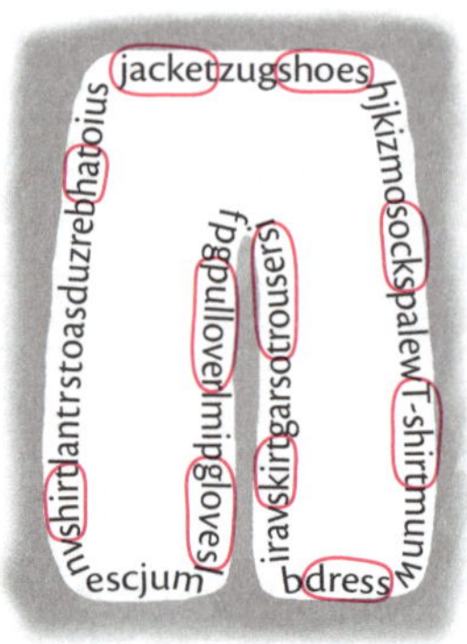

trousers
gloves
skirt
pullover
dress
shirt
socks
T-shirt
shoes
jacket
hat

zu 1: Verbinde die Wörter mit den passenden Bildern. Umkreise das überflüssige Wort und schreibe es auf.
zu 2: Finde die Wörter zu den Abbildungen, umkreise und schreibe sie auf.

3 Read and colour.

Kate is wearing an orange jacket, blue trousers and green gloves.

Samir is wearing a yellow jacket, green shoes and a grey hat.

Harry is wearing a black hat, yellow gloves, and red trousers.

Emily is wearing a green jacket, brown shoes and a pink pullover.

4 One word is wrong. Circle and write.

socks	(blue)	shirt	hat	blue
yellow	pink	(skirt)	green	skirt
hat	(grey)	shirt	shoes	grey
(shirt)	green	yellow	white	shirt
trousers	jacket	pullover	(brown)	brown
jeans	(black)	T-shirt	cap	black

zu 3: Lies die Texte und male die Kleidungsstücke der Kinder dazu passend an.
zu 4: Umkreise in jeder Zeile das nicht passende Wort und schreibe es auf.

5 Read and tick (✓).

He is wearing
- [ ] a black jacket, an orange hat and green gloves.
- [ ] a white hat, blue gloves and a pink jacket.
- [x] green gloves, a pink hat and a blue jacket.

She is wearing
- [x] red shoes, black trousers and a yellow pullover.
- [ ] red trousers, a yellow pullover and blue shoes.
- [ ] a green pullover, pink trousers and brown shoes.

6 What clothes can you see? Write.

I can see black trousers, white socks, brown shoes, yellow gloves, a blue shirt, a red skirt, a pink dress, a yellow pullover, a grey jacket, a green hat and an orange T-shirt.

zu 5: Finde heraus, wie die Sätze richtig heißen und hake ab.
zu 6: Schreibe die Wörter für die Kleidung und deren Farben auf.

7 Read and draw lines.

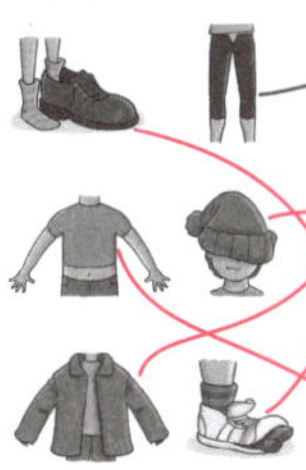

The black trousers are
The blue jacket is
The pink hat is
The yellow shoe is
The red shoe is
The orange T-shirt is

too big.
too small.

8 Write. Draw the smiley.

☺ Yes, I do.
☹ No, I don't.

Do you like the green T-shirt? — Yes, I do. ☺

Do you like the brown shoes? — No, I don't. ☹

Do you like the blue hat? — ______

zu 7: Bilde Sätze zu den Bildern.
zu 8: Schreibe die zu den Bildern passenden Texte in die Sprechblasen. Male zum letzten Bild einen Smiley deiner Wahl und ergänze die Sprechblasen.

9 Write.

I'm wearing blue shoes, a red skirt, and a white T-shirt.

I'm wearing black trousers, a yellow shirt and green shoes.

10 Read and colour.

four grey pullovers | five orange T-shirts | two red shirts
three green skirts | one blue jacket | twelve yellow socks

zu 9: Schreibe auf, welche Kleidungsstücke die Kinder tragen.
zu 10: Male die Bilder passend zu den Texten an.

11 Write.

s r e d s	dress	o c s k s	socks
i h s t r	shirt	t k j c a e	jacket
e v r o u l p l	pullover	a t h	hat
s r e t r u o s	trousers	e h o s s	shoes

Draw lines.

The trousers are	in	the school bag.
The dress is	next to	the cat.
The pullover is	on	the bike.
The socks are	under	the dog.
The shoes are	behind	the pencil case.
The hat is	in front of	the scissors.

zu 11: Ordne die Buchstaben und schreibe die (Kleidungs-)Wörter richtig auf.
zu Extra: Bilde Sätze zu den Bildern.

1 Number. Find the extra picture.

1. listening to music
2. meeting friends
3. playing computer games
4. playing football
5. reading
6. watching TV

6, 3, 5, 2, 4, 1

2 Write.

WATCHING TV	READING
PLAYING FOOTBALL	PLAYING COMPUTER GAMES
MEETING FRIENDS	LISTENING TO MUSIC

zu 1: Nummeriere die Bilder passend zu den Wörtern und umkreise das überflüssige Bild.
zu 2: Schreibe die Wörter zu den Freizeitaktivitäten auf.

3 Draw lines and smileys.

I like meeting friends.
I don't like playing football.
I like watching TV.
I don't like reading.
I don't like playing computer games.
I like listening to music.

4 Find the hobbies. Write.

Tim: I like watching TV.
Lisa: I like playing football.
Bob: I like reading.
Ella: I like listening to music.

zu 3: Verbinde die Sätze mit den passenden Bildern und zeichne die richtigen Smileys dazu.
zu 4: Fahre die Linien nach und schreibe Sätze zu den Hobbys der Kinder.

5 Write.

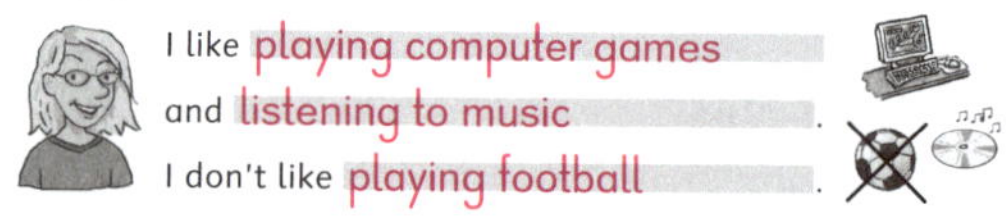

I like playing computer games
and listening to music.
I don't like playing football.

I like reading
and meeting friends.
I don't like watching TV.

6 Number and draw smileys. That's boring. Great idea!

1	2	3	4

4	What about playing football?	That's boring!
2	What about playing computer games?	Great idea!
1	What about reading a storybook?	That's boring!
3	What about meeting friends?	Great idea!

zu 5: Ergänze die Sätze zu den Hobbys der Kinder.
zu 6: Nummeriere die Dialoge passend zu den Bildern und zeichne die richtigen Smileys dazu.

7 Number.

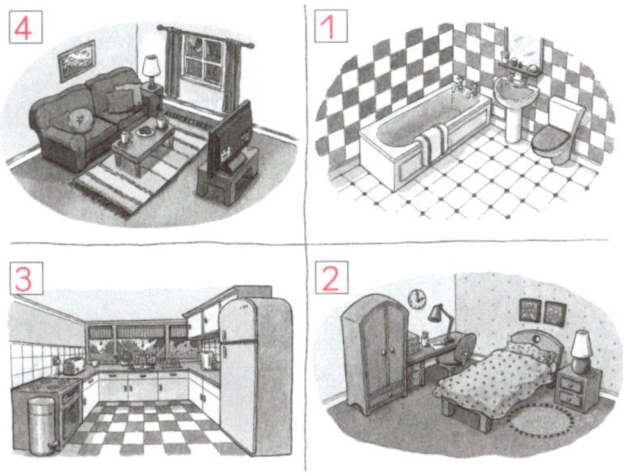

(1) bathroom (2) bedroom (3) kitchen (4) living room

8 Write.

ambtroho	bathroom
gnlivi ormo	living room
eckihnt	kitchen
erobmod	bedroom

zu 7: Nummeriere die Bilder passend zu den Wörtern.
zu 8: Ordne die Buchstaben und schreibe die Wörter für die Räume richtig auf.

9 Find the words. Write.

bed · chair · lamp · sofa · table · wardrobe

R	F	T	L	P	B	X	A
O	S	L	A	M	P	M	B
N	C	P	C	Q	V	T	I
O	H	G	E	X	C	A	W
W	A	R	D	R	O	B	E
N	I	I	E	S	M	L	A
R	R	L	J	N	B	E	D
H	L	S	O	F	A	K	O

sofa
table
wardrobe
lamp
chair
bed

10 Read, colour and write.

The sofa is green.
The wardrobe is yellow.
The table is brown.
The chair is blue.
The bed is grey.
The lamp is red.

zu 9: Finde die Wörter im Suchworträtsel und schreibe sie auf.
zu 10: Lies die Sätze und male die Gegenstände dazu passend an. Ergänze die Wörter für die Farben und Möbel passend zu den Bildern.

11 Right or wrong? Read and tick (✓) the right answers.

- [x] There is a green pullover in the bathroom.
- [ ] There is a rat in the bathroom.
- [ ] There is a wardrobe in the kitchen.
- [x] There is a lamp in the bedroom.
- [x] There are books in the living room.
- [ ] There is a blue bed in the bedroom.

☆ Write the furniture words.

In Emily's bedroom,
there is a table,
there is a bed,
there is a chair,
there is a wardrobe
and there is a lamp.
There isn't a sofa.

zu 11: Lies die Sätze zum Bild und hake die richtigen Aussagen ab.
zu Extra: Schreibe auf, welche Möbelstücke im Bild zu sehen sind und welches Möbelstück fehlt.

1 Draw lines. Find the extra word.

strawberry
cherry lemon
banana plum
orange apple
chocolate
peach

The word chocolate is extra.

2 Write.

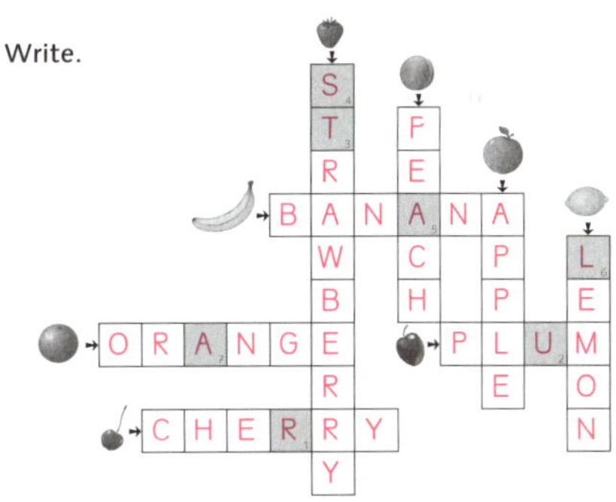

					S						
					T		F				
					R		E				
				B	A	N	A	N	A		
					W		C		P		L
					B		H		P		E
O	R	A	N	G	E			P	L	U	M
					R				E		O
	C	H	E	R	R	Y					N
					Y						

Solution: F R U I T ■ S A L A D

zu 1: Verbinde die Wörter mit den richtigen Bildern. Umkreise das überflüssige Wort und schreibe es auf.
zu 2: Schreibe die Wörter auf. Finde das Lösungswort.

3 Read, number and write.

1. I like cherry juice and orange juice.
   I don't like plum juice. My name is Greg.
2. I like peach juice and cherry juice.
   I don't like lemon juice. My name is Sally.
3. I like apple juice and orange juice.
   I don't like strawberry juice. My name is Sam.
4. I like lemon juice and strawberry juice.
   I don't like banana milk. My name is Jane.

4 Write.

- Do you like chocolate ice cream? – Yes, I do.
- Do you like strawberry ice cream? – No, I don't.
- Do you like lemon ice cream? – No, I don't.
- Do you like banana ice cream? – Yes, I do.
- Do you like orange ice cream? – Yes, I do.
- Do you like cherry ice cream? – No, I don't.

zu 3: Ordne die Sätze den passenden Bildern zu und nummeriere die Bilder. Ergänze die Sätze.
zu 4: Ergänze die Sätze passend zu den Bildern.

5 Draw lines. Find the extra word.

60, 15, 100, 40, 20, 70

forty, twenty, seventy, fifty, ninety, fifteen

thirty, sixty, eighty, twelve, ten, one hundred, forty-five

10, 30, 50, 80, 45, 90

The word twelve is extra.

6 Read, colour and write.

Ten is blue.
Sixty is red.
Ninety is orange.
Fifty is black.
One hundred is yellow.

20 80
70 45
40 10
100 50
60 30
90

Thirty is grey.
Seventy is brown.
Forty is green.
Eighty is white.
Twenty is pink.

Forty-five is yellow and orange.

zu 5: Verbinde die Wörter mit den passenden Zahlen. Umkreise das überflüssige Wort und schreibe es auf.
zu 6: Lies die Sätze und male die Zahlen richtig an. Ergänze den Satz.

7 Read and number.

2 I'd like an orange juice, please.
4 Thank you. Bye.
1 Hi, can I help you?
3 That's 50 p.

3 Good idea! A chocolate ice cream for me, please.
1 I'm hot.
4 And a lemon ice cream for me.
2 What about some ice cream?

8 Read and tick (✓) the right answers.

- [x] Strawberry juice is £ 1.50.
- [ ] A banana is 70 p.
- [ ] The oranges are blue.
- [ ] Cherry juice is £ 1.60.
- [x] Banana milk is 90 p.
- [x] They don't have water.
- [x] An orange is 45 p.
- [ ] There are worms in the basket.
- [x] Peach juice is £ 1.10.
- [ ] There are four bananas in the box.

zu 7: Nummeriere die Dialoge in der richtigen Reihenfolge.
zu 8: Lies die Sätze zum Bild und hake die richtigen Aussagen ab.

9 Write and draw lines.

How much is the skateboard?
The skateboard is twenty pounds.

How much are the trousers?
The trousers are fifteen pounds.

How much is the book?
The book is five pounds.

How much are the pencils?
The pencils are two pounds.

10 Write the shopping lists.

1 apple
1 rubber
1 football
1 cherry ice cream

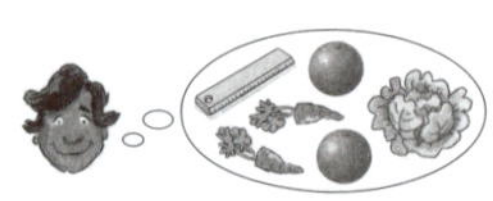

2 oranges
1 ruler
2 carrots
1 lettuce

zu 9: Ergänze die Sätze und schreibe die richtigen Preise auf die Schilder. Verbinde die Sätze mit den passenden Bildern.
zu 10: Schreibe die Einkaufslisten.

11 Find the prices. Write.

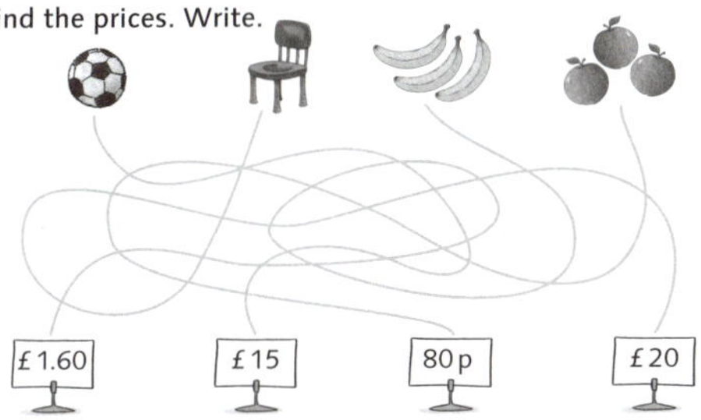

How much is the football? It's £15.
How much is the chair? It's £20.
How much are the bananas? They are £1.60.
How much are the apples? They are 80p.

Read and number.

3 Emily buys four ice creams.
5 "Where's Emily?", Samir asks.
2 They all want ice cream.
1 Emily and her friends are in the park. It's hot.
4 Oh no! There is ice cream everywhere!

zu 11: Fahre die Linien nach und schreibe Dialoge zu den Preisen der Gegenstände auf.
zu Extra: Nummeriere die Sätze passend zu den Bildern.

1 Write.

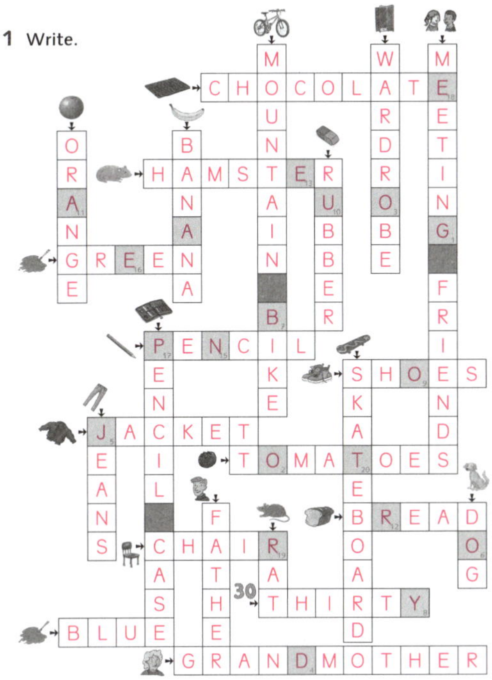

Solution: G O O D J O B !
Y O U A R E A N E X P E R T !

zu 1: Schreibe die Wörter auf. Finde die Lösung.

2 Read, draw and write.

My favourite …
colour: red
pet: rabbit
hobby: digging
food: worms

name: Mr Mole

My favourite …
colour: ______
pet: ______
hobby: ______
food: ______

name: ______

Hi, I'm Mr Mole. What's your name?

My name is ______. What's your favourite colour, Mr Mole?

My favourite colour is red. What's your favourite colour?

My favourite colour is ______. What's your favourite pet?

My favourite pet is a rabbit. What about you?

My favourite pet is a ______. Have you got a hobby?

Yes. My hobby is digging. What about you? What do you like doing in your free time?

I like ______. What have you got in your lunch box? I've got ______ in my lunch box.

I've got worms in my lunch box! That's my favourite food!

zu 2: Gestalte deinen Steckbrief. Ergänze die Sprechblasen passend zu den Steckbriefen.

So kannst du bequem und mit Spaß Wörter lernen:

- Schreibe englische Wörter auf (Haft-) Zettel. Klebe die Zettel auf Gegenstände in deinem Zimmer.

- Suche Bilder, die zu deinen englischen Wörtern passen. Schreibe die Wörter auf (Haft-)Zettel, klebe diese auf die Bilder und hänge beides zusammen auf.

- Schreibe englische Wörter auf große Blätter und male eigene Bilder dazu. Verteile die Blätter in deinem Zimmer (oder in der Wohnung, wenn deine Eltern einverstanden sind!)

So siehst du die Wörter immer wieder!

- Erstelle Wortnetze (*word webs*) zu den Themen deines Englischunterrichts. Schreibe darin alle Wörter auf, die du zu einem Thema kennst. Später kannst du immer wieder neue, passende Wörter ergänzen.

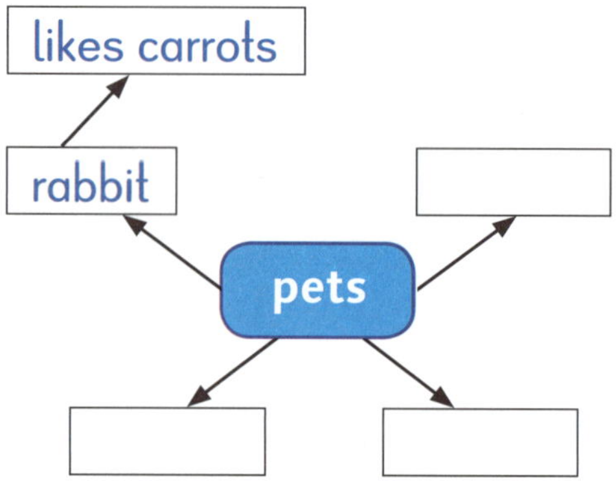

Suche dir für jeden Tag einen Tipp aus und wiederhole einige Wörter. Je häufiger du deine Wörter übst, desto besser kannst du sie dir merken!

Hier kannst du deine Wörter üben:

Hier kannst du deine Wörter üben:

Hier kannst du deine Wörter üben:

Liebe Eltern, liebe Lehrkraft,

mit dem *Sunshine Word Trainer* ermöglichen Sie den Kindern schon früh, die wichtigsten Wörter und Inhalte des Englischunterrichts selbstständig und gezielt zu üben und zu vertiefen. Die Aufgaben sind leicht nachvollziehbar und selbsterklärend. Mithilfe der Lösungen überprüfen die Kinder ihre Ergebnisse eigenständig. Somit können sie sowohl in der Schule als auch am Nachmittag zu Hause, ihre Englischkenntnisse ohne helfende Begleitung sichern.
Auf diese Weise wird der Unterricht sinnvoll ergänzt. Die spielerischen Aufgabenformate fördern, zusammen mit der Belohnungsseite, die Motivation der Kinder beim Lösen der Aufgaben.

Passgenau zum Lehrwerk behandeln die Kapitel des *Word Trainers* die wichtigsten Inhalte der *Sunshine*-Units. Unterschiedliche Wortfelder werden innerhalb des *Word Trainers* wiederholt aufgegriffen. Anhand von abwechslungsreichen, den Kindern aus *Sunshine* weitgehend bekannten und beliebten Übungsformen werden Wortfelder miteinander verknüpft. So wird das Vokabelwissen der Kinder nachhaltig und altersgerecht im Gedächtnis verankert. Der beliebte Begleiter Mr Mole ist an ihrer Seite, wenn die Schülerinnen und Schüler intuitiv und ohne weiteren Erklärungsaufwand mit dem *Word Trainer* spielerisch und lehrplangerecht ihr Wissen sichern.

Das schafft eine solide Basis für das weitere Englischlernen!

5 Read and tick (✓).

He is wearing

- ☐ a black jacket, an orange hat and green gloves.
- ☐ a white hat, blue gloves and a pink jacket.
- ☐ green gloves, a pink hat and a blue jacket.

She is wearing

- ☐ red shoes, black trousers and a yellow pullover.
- ☐ red trousers, a yellow pullover and blue shoes.
- ☐ a green pullover, pink trousers and brown shoes.

6 What clothes can you see? Write.

I can see black trousers,
white ____,
brown ____,
____ ____, a ____
____, a ____ ____,
a ____ ____, a ____
____, a ____ ____,
a ____ ____ and
an orange ____.

zu 5: Finde heraus, wie die Sätze richtig heißen und hake ab.
zu 6: Schreibe die Wörter für die Kleidung und deren Farben auf.

7 Read and draw lines.

The black trousers are

The blue jacket is

The pink hat is

The yellow shoe is

The red shoe is

The orange T-shirt is

too big.

too small.

8 Write. Draw the smiley.

Yes, I do.

No, I don't.

Do you like the green T-shirt?

Yes, ______

zu 7: Bilde Sätze zu den Bildern.

zu 8: Schreibe die zu den Bildern passenden Texte in die Sprechblasen. Male zum letzten Bild einen Smiley deiner Wahl und ergänze die Sprechblasen.

9 Write.

I'm wearing blue shoes,
a ______________________,
and a ______________________.

I'm wearing black ______________,
a ______________________,
and ______________________.

10 Read and colour.

four grey pullovers | five orange T-shirts | two red shirts
three green skirts | one blue jacket | twelve yellow socks

11 Write.

s r e ds		o c s k s	
i h s t r		t k j c a e	
e v r o u l p l		a t h	
s r e t r u o s		e h o s s	

Draw lines.

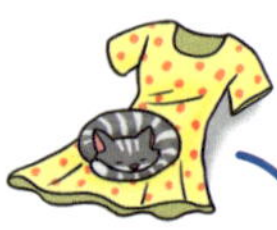	The trousers are	in	the school bag.
	The dress is	next to	the cat.
	The pullover is	on	the bike.
	The socks are	under	the dog.
	The shoes are	behind	the pencil case.
	The hat is	in front of	the scissors.

zu 11: Ordne die Buchstaben und schreibe die (Kleidungs-)Wörter richtig auf.
zu Extra: Bilde Sätze zu den Bildern.

Free-time activities

hobbies **5**

1 Number. Find the extra picture.

(1) listening to music
(2) meeting friends
(3) playing computer games
(4) playing football
(5) reading
(6) watching TV

2 Write.

WATCHING TV

READING

PLAYING FOOTBALL

PLAYING COMPUTER GAMES

MEETING FRIENDS

LISTENING TO MUSIC

zu 1: Nummeriere die Bilder passend zu den Wörtern und umkreise das überflüssige Bild.
zu 2: Schreibe die Wörter zu den Freizeitaktivitäten auf.

3 Draw lines and smileys. ☺ ☹

I like meeting friends.

I don't like playing football.

I like watching TV.

I don't like reading.

I don't like playing computer games.

I like listening to music.

4 Find the hobbies. Write.

Tim: I like ______________________.

Lisa: I ______________________.

Bob: ______________________.

Ella: ______________________.

zu 3: Verbinde die Sätze mit den passenden Bildern und zeichne die richtigen Smileys dazu.
zu 4: Fahre die Linien nach und schreibe Sätze zu den Hobbys der Kinder.

5 Write.

I like ______

and ______.

I don't like ______.

I like ______

and ______.

I don't like ______.

6 Number and draw smileys.

☹ That's boring.	☺ Great idea!

1	2	3	4

4 — What about playing football? — That's boring!

☐ — What about playing computer games? — Great idea!

☐ — What about reading a storybook? — That's boring!

☐ — What about meeting friends? — Great idea!

zu 5: Ergänze die Sätze zu den Hobbys der Kinder.
zu 6: Nummeriere die Dialoge passend zu den Bildern und zeichne die richtigen Smileys dazu.

7 Number.

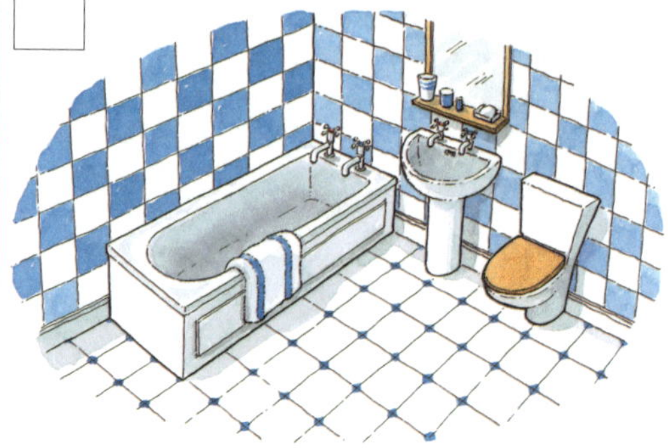

(1) bathroom (2) bedroom (3) kitchen (4) living room

8 Write.

ambtroho ______

gnlivi ormo ______

eckihnt ______

erobmod ______

zu 7: Nummeriere die Bilder passend zu den Wörtern.
zu 8: Ordne die Buchstaben und schreibe die Wörter für die Räume richtig auf.

9 Find the words. Write.

bed · chair · lamp · sofa · table · wardrobe

→ ↓

R	F	T	L	P	B	X	A
O	S	L	A	M	P	M	B
N	C	P	C	Q	V	T	I
O	H	G	E	X	C	A	W
W	A	R	D	R	O	B	E
N	I	I	E	S	M	L	A
R	R	L	J	N	B	E	D
H	L	S	O	F	A	K	O

 ____________

 ____________

 ____________

 ____________

 ____________

 ____________

10 Read, colour and write.

The sofa is green.

The wardrobe is yellow.

The ____________ is brown.

The chair is ____________.

The ____________ is grey.

The ____________ is ____________.

zu 9: Finde die Wörter im Suchworträtsel und schreibe sie auf.
zu 10: Lies die Sätze und male die Gegenstände dazu passend an. Ergänze die Wörter für die Farben und Möbel passend zu den Bildern.

11 Right or wrong? Read and tick (✓) the right answers.

- [x] There is a green pullover in the bathroom.
- [ ] There is a rat in the bathroom.
- [ ] There is a wardrobe in the kitchen.
- [ ] There is a lamp in the bedroom.
- [ ] There are books in the living room.
- [ ] There is a blue bed in the bedroom.

Write the furniture words.

In Emily's bedroom,

there is a table,

there is ____________,

there ____________,

____

and ____________.

There isn't a ____________.

zu 11: Lies die Sätze zum Bild und hake die richtigen Aussagen ab.
zu Extra: Schreibe auf, welche Möbelstücke im Bild zu sehen sind und welches Möbelstück fehlt.

1 Draw lines. Find the extra word.

strawberry

cherry lemon

banana plum

orange apple

chocolate

peach

The word ______________ is extra.

2 Write.

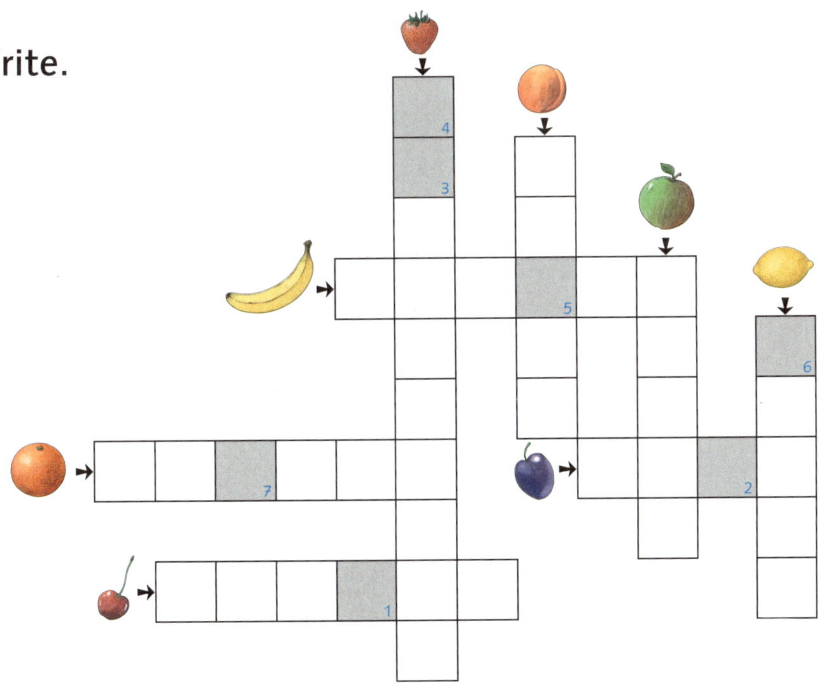

Solution: F _ _ I _ ■ _ _ _ _ D

1 2 3 4 5 6 7

zu 1: Verbinde die Wörter mit den richtigen Bildern. Umkreise das überflüssige Wort und schreibe es auf.
zu 2: Schreibe die Wörter auf. Finde das Lösungswort.

3 Read, number and write.

Sally ☐ Jane ☐ Sam ☐ Greg ☐

(1) I like cherry juice and ______ juice.
I don't like plum juice. My name is ______.

(2) I like peach juice and ______ juice.
I don't like ______ juice. My name is ______.

(3) I like ______ and ______.
I don't like strawberry juice. My name is ______.

(4) I like ______ and ______.
I don't like ______ milk. My name is ______.

4 Write.

Do you like chocolate ice cream? — Yes, I do.

Do you like strawberry ______? — No, I don't.

Do you like ______? — No, ______.

Do you ______? — Yes, ______.

______? — ______

______? — ______

zu 3: Ordne die Sätze den passenden Bildern zu und nummeriere die Bilder. Ergänze die Sätze.
zu 4: Ergänze die Sätze passend zu den Bildern.

5 Draw lines. Find the extra word.

60, 15, 100, 40, 20, 70

forty, thirty, twenty, sixty, eighty, seventy, twelve, fifty, ten, ninety, one hundred, fifteen, forty-five

10, 30, 50, 80, 45, 90

The word ______ is extra.

6 Read, colour and write.

Ten is blue.

Sixty is red.

Ninety is orange.

Fifty is black.

One hundred is yellow.

20 80
70 45
40 10
100 50
60 30
90

Thirty is grey.

Seventy is brown.

Forty is green.

Eighty is white.

Twenty is pink.

Forty-five is ______ and ______.

zu 5: Verbinde die Wörter mit den passenden Zahlen. Umkreise das überflüssige Wort und schreibe es auf.
zu 6: Lies die Sätze und male die Zahlen richtig an. Ergänze den Satz.

7 Read and number.

- [ ] I'd like an orange juice, please.
- [ ] Thank you. Bye.
- [ ] Hi, can I help you?
- [ ] That's 50 p.

- [ ] Good idea! A chocolate ice cream for me, please.
- [ ] I'm hot.
- [ ] And a lemon ice cream for me.
- [ ] What about some ice cream?

8 Read and tick (✓) the right answers.

- [x] Strawberry juice is £ 1.50.
- [ ] A banana is 70 p.
- [ ] The oranges are blue.
- [ ] Cherry juice is £ 1.60.
- [ ] Banana milk is 90 p.
- [ ] They don't have water.
- [ ] An orange is 45 p.
- [ ] There are worms in the basket.
- [ ] Peach juice is £ 1.10.
- [ ] There are four bananas in the box.

zu 7: Nummeriere die Dialoge in der richtigen Reihenfolge.
zu 8: Lies die Sätze zum Bild und hake die richtigen Aussagen ab.

9 Write and draw lines.

How much is the skateboard?

The __________ is twenty pounds.

How much are the __________?

The trousers are fifteen pounds.

How much is the book?

The __________ is five pounds.

How much are the __________?

The pencils are two pounds.

10 Write the shopping lists.

1 apple

2 oranges

11 Find the prices. Write.

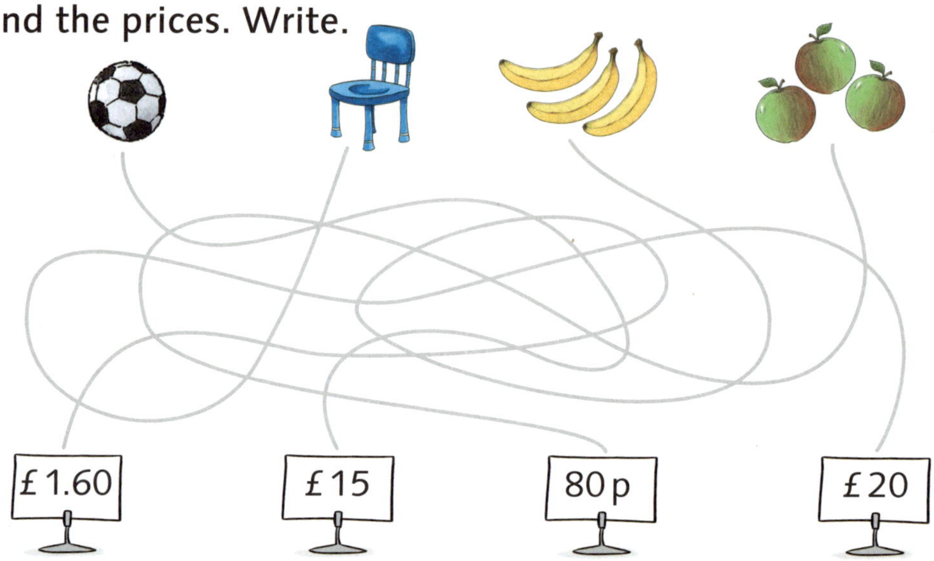

How much is the football? It's ________.

________ the chair? ________.

________ are the bananas? They are ________.

________ the apples? ________.

Read and number.

☐ Emily buys four ice creams.

☐ "Where's Emily?", Samir asks.

☐ They all want ice cream.

☐ Emily and her friends are in the park. It's hot.

☐ Oh no! There is ice cream everywhere!

zu 11: Fahre die Linien nach und schreibe Dialoge zu den Preisen der Gegenstände auf.
zu Extra: Nummeriere die Sätze passend zu den Bildern.

1 Write.

Solution:

1	2	3	4	■	5	6	7	!

8	9	10	■	11	12	13	■	14	15	■	16	X	17	18	19	20	!
												X					

zu 1: Schreibe die Wörter auf. Finde die Lösung.

What I can do and say

2 Read, draw and write.

My favourite ... ♥
colour: red
pet: rabbit
hobby: digging
food: worms

name: Mr Mole

My favourite ... ♥
colour: ______
pet: ______
hobby: ______
food: ______

name: ______

Hi, I'm Mr Mole. What's your name?

My name is ______. What's your favourite colour, Mr Mole?

My ______ ______. What's your favourite colour?

My ______ ______. What's your favourite pet?

My ______ is a ______. What about you?

My ______ ______. Have you got a hobby?

Yes. My hobby is ______. What about you? What do you like doing in your free time?

I like ______. What have you got in your lunch box? I've got ______ ______ in my lunch box.

I've got ______ in my lunch box! That's my favourite food!

zu 2: Gestalte deinen Steckbrief. Ergänze die Sprechblasen passend zu den Steckbriefen.

Colours

black schwarz

blue blau

brown braun

green grün

grey grau

orange orange

pink rosa

red rot

white weiß

yellow gelb

What's your favourite colour?

My favourite colour is red.

More words:

Family

brother Bruder

father Vater

grandfather Großvater

grandmother Großmutter

mother Mutter

sister Schwester

Have you got brothers or sisters?

No, I haven't.

Yes, I have. I've got a sister. She is nine.

More words:

My words

Pets

 **cat** Katze

 **dog** Hund

 **fish** Fisch

 **guinea pig** Meerschweinchen

 **hamster** Hamster

 **mouse** Maus

 **rabbit** Kaninchen

 **rat** Ratte

What's your favourite pet?

My favourite pet is a dog.

More words:

____

____

Food

 **apple** Apfel

 **bread** Brot

 **carrot** Karotte

 **lettuce** (Kopf-)Salat

 **peanuts** Erdnüsse

 **tomato** Tomate

What do you like?

I like apples.

I like carrots. I don't like peanuts.

More words:

____

____

My words

School things

 **book** Buch

 **felt tip** Filzstift

 **glue stick** Klebestift

 **lunch box** Brotdose

 **pen** Füller

 **pencil** Bleistift

 **pencil case** Federmappe

 **pencil sharpener** Anspitzer

 **rubber** Radiergummi

 **ruler** Lineal

 **school bag** Schultasche

 **scissors** Schere

Can I have your ruler, please?

Sorry, I haven't got a ruler.

Yes, you can. Here you are.

More words:

Clothes

 **dress** Kleid

 **gloves** Handschuhe

 **hat** Mütze

 **jacket** Jacke

 **pullover** Pullover

 **shirt** Hemd

 **shoes** Schuhe

 **skirt** Rock

 **socks** Socken

 **T-shirt** T-Shirt

 **trousers** Hose

What are you wearing?

I'm wearing a blue T-shirt.

More words:

My words

Hobbies

 **listening to music** Musik hören

 **meeting friends** Freunde treffen

 **playing computer games** Computerspiele spielen

 **playing football** Fuβball spielen

 **reading** lesen

 **watching TV** fernsehen

Do you like reading?

Yes, I do. I like reading.

What about playing football?

Playing football is boring!

More words:

Rooms and furniture

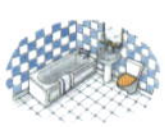 **bathroom** Badezimmer

 **bedroom** Schlafzimmer

 **kitchen** Küche

 **living room** Wohnzimmer

Is there a bed in the kitchen?

No, there isn't. There is a bed in the bedroom.

 **bed** Bett

 **chair** Stuhl

 **lamp** Lampe

 **table** Tisch

 **wardrobe** Schrank

More words:

Fruit and drinks

apple Apfel
banana Banane
cherry Kirsche
juice Saft
lemon Zitrone
milk Milch
orange Orange
peach Pfirsich
plum Pflaume
strawberry Erdbeere

I'm thirsty.
What about some orange juice?

I'm hungry.
What about a banana?

More words:

Numbers

1 **one** eins
2 **two** zwei
3 **three** drei
4 **four** vier
5 **five** fünf
6 **six** sechs
7 **seven** sieben
8 **eight** acht
9 **nine** neun
10 **ten** zehn

11 **eleven** elf
12 **twelve** zwölf
13 **thirteen** dreizehn
14 **fourteen** vierzehn
15 **fifteen** fünfzehn
16 **sixteen** sechzehn
17 **seventeen** siebzehn
18 **eighteen** achtzehn
19 **nineteen** neunzehn
20 **twenty** zwanzig

10 **ten** zehn
20 **twenty** zwanzig
30 **thirty** dreiβig
40 **forty** vierzig
50 **fifty** fünfzig
60 **sixty** sechzig
70 **seventy** siebzig
80 **eighty** achtzig
90 **ninety** neunzig
100 **one hundred** hundert

Sunshine

Lehrwerk für den früh beginnenden Englischunterricht

Mr Mole's Word Trainer 3

Erarbeitet von

Daniela Röbers, Erkelenz; Caroline Schröder, München

Auf der Grundlage der Ausgabe von

Birgit Hollbrügge, Bielefeld; Ulrike Kraaz, Werther

Beratende Mitwirkung

Wolfgang Gehring, Aschaffenburg; Renate Hafner, Blaustein

Verlagsredaktion

Daniela Aue

Illustration

Maria Aurelio, Berlin; Christian Bartz, Berlin; Beehive Illustration, Cirencester, England: Neil Chapman, Mike Phillipps; Raimo Bergt, Berlin; Volker Fredrich, Hamburg; Mary Hall, Bath, England; Jan Lewis, Pangbourne, England; Katharina Wieker, Berlin; Dorothee Wolters, Köln

Gesamtgestaltung

Corinna Babylon, Berlin

Technische Umsetzung

Michaela Müller für Corngreen GmbH, Leipzig

www.cornelsen.de

1. Auflage, 1. Druck 2018

Alle Drucke dieser Auflage sind inhaltlich unverändert und können im Unterricht nebeneinander verwendet werden.

Druck: H. Heenemann, Berlin

ISBN 978-3-06-084250-6

PEFC
PEFC/04-31-1156

PEFC zertifiziert
Dieses Produkt stammt aus nachhaltig bewirtschafteten Wäldern und kontrollierten Quellen.

www.pefc.de

Quellenangaben

Kapitelicons

Kind: GlowImages/Westend61; Hand: Fotolia/Vitalinko; Familie: GlowImage; Rollschuh: Clip Dealer/Harald Fila; Tomate: Fotolia/food pictures studio; Hund: Fotolia/grafikplus-foto; Schreibende Hand: Mauritius images/Alamy; Rucksack: Fotolia/design56; Füße: Mauritius images/Photoshot Creative/Stuart Cox; Kleid: Fotolia/Alexandra Karamyshev; Stuhl: Fotolia/Vely; Fußball: Fotolia/Andrey Kiselev; Erdbeere: Fotolia/PeJo; Geld: Fotolia/Comugnero Silvana; Kerzen: Fotolia/Ruth Black; Zweig: Your photo today. A1 pix – superbild; Muffin: Mauritius images/Alamy; Ostereier: Okapia/© Creativ Studio Heinemann/imageBROKER

Illustrationen

MARIA AURELIO S. 39/Lösungsteil: Notizzettel | CHRISTIAN BARTZ S. 10 (u.); S. 15: Würmer; S. 20 (u.); S. 23 (u.): Hose mit Buchstaben; S. 25 (o.); S. 26 (o.); S. 27 (o.); S. 28; S. 36: Mr Mole mit Kaninchen; S. 39/40: Preisschilder; S. 47: Milch, Saft; Innenumschlag, vorne; Lösungsteil: schreibende Hand | RAIMO BERGT S. 17/18 (u.)/20 (o.)/45: Buch, Federmappe (blau), Lineal, Radiergummi, Schere, Schultasche; S. 23/25/45 (u.): Handschuhe, Hose, Jacke, Kleid, Mütze, Pullover, Rock, Schuhe, Socken, T-Shirt; S. 26: Mütze, Schuhe, T-Shirt; S. 27 (u.): Pullover; S. 37/47: Zahlen; S. 39: Hose, Lineal, Radiergummi; S. 41: dreißig, Jacke, Jeans, Federmappe, Radiergummi, Schuhe; Lösungsteil: T-Shirt | NEIL CHAPMAN S. 9: Köpfe (Emily, Kate, Samir); S. 13 (u.): Hamster, Hund, Kaninchen, Katze; S. 14 (o.): Salat, Karotte, Apfel, Erdnüsse; S. 14 (u.): Äpfel, Erdnüsse, Karotten, Kopfsalat; S. 15 (außer Mr Mole u. Würmer); S. 16: Erdnüsse, Hamster, Karotten, Kinder; S. 21 (o.): Buch, Hand mit Bleistift/Filzstift/Füller; S. 23/25/45 (u.): Hemd; S. 24; S. 26: Kinder; S. 27 (u.): Hemd, Rock, T-Shirt; S. 30 (o.): Bild 1–5; S. 34 (o.); S. 36 (o.): Trinkpäckchen; S. 38; S. 39: Karotten, Salat; S. 40 (u.): Bild 1, 3, 5; S. 44 (u.): Apfel, Erdnüsse, Karotte, Salat; Lösungsteil: Kalender | VOLKER FREDRICH S. 3: Maulwürfe; S. 7: Inlineskates, Mr Mole mit Fahrrad; S. 8/9 (außer Köpfe: Emily, Kate, Samir); S. 10 (o.); S. 11 (außer u.: Maus und Hamster); S. 12/13 (o.); S. 13 (u.): Maus; S. 14 (o.)/44: Brot, Tomate; S. 16 (o.): Kaninchen; S. 18 (o.); S. 19: Mr Mole; S. 21: Kinder, Mr Mole; S. 22 (u.); S. 29 (o.): Bild 1, 3/(u.): Bild 1, 3, 6; S. 30 (o.): Bild 6/(u.); S. 31: CD, Fußball, Kinder, TV; S. 32 (u.): Mr Mole; S. 34 (u.); S. 36 (o.): Kinder; S. 37: Mr Mole; S. 38: Eis in Sprechblase; S. 39: Fußball, Mr Mole; S. 40: Fußball/Bild 2, 4 (u.); S. 41: Brot, Großmutter, Tomate, Vater; S. 43: Familienbilder; S. 46: CD, Fußball, Fernseher; Kapitel-Motive (außer Mr Mole im Liegestuhl); Innenumschlag, hinten; Lösungsteil: Mr Mole | MARY HALL S. 3: weißes Kaninchen; S. 4/5; S. 7: Fahrrad, Roller, Skateboard; S. 11: Hamster, Maus; S. 15/16/35: Mr Mole; S. 17/18/20/45: Anspitzer, Bleistift, Brotdose, Filzstift, Füller, Klebestift; S. 19: Lineal; S. 29: Bild 2-6 (o.)/Bild 2, 4, 5 (u.); S. 31: Buch, Computer, Mr Mole, zwei Kinder; S. 32 (o.)/46 (u.): Badezimmer, Schlafzimmer, Küche; S. 35/36 (o.)/47: Apfel, Banane, Erdbeere, Kirsche, Orange, Pfirsich, Zitrone; S. 39: Apfel, Bleistifte, Buch, Orangen, Skateboard; S. 40: Bananen, Äpfel; S. 41: Banane, Bleistift, Fahrrad, Farben (blau, grün), Freunde, Hamster, Hund, Orange, Ratte, Skateboard; S. 43: Farbklekse; S. 44 (Tiere außer Fisch); S. 46 (o.): wie S. 29 (u.); Kapitel-Motiv: Mr Mole im Liegestuhl | JAN LEWIS: S. 3/21/Lösungsteil: Rahmen | MIKE PHILLIPPS S. 36/39: Eisbecher | KATHARINA WIEKER S. 32/46: Wohnzimmer; S. 33; S. 35/36/47: Pflaume; S. 40: Stuhl; S. 41: Schokolade, Schrank, Stuhl; S. 44: Fisch; S. 46: Bett, Lampe, Schrank, Stuhl, Tisch; Lösungsteil: Stuhl | DOROTHEE WOLTERS S. 6; S. 13 (u.): Fisch; S. 14 (u.): Tomate; S. 22 (o.): Mäuse; S. 27 (u.): Jacke, Socken